FORCES

Written by
Chris Oxlade

Illustrated by
Siân Frances, Janos Marffy, Tracey Wilson

Edited by
Katherine James

Designed by
Steve Hollingshead

Picture research by
Frances Abraham

CONTENTS

Forces everywhere

When you ride your bike, throw a ball, or simply move about, you use forces. A force is a push or a pull. When you ride your bike, you push on the pedals. When you throw a ball, your hand pushes the ball. When you walk about, your feet push on the ground.

As you cycle along, your hair moves in the wind. The moving air makes the force.

When you sit on the seat, you push down on it. Your weight makes the force. It squashes the padding in the seat.

To make a bicycle move, you push down on the pedals with your feet. Your leg muscles make the pushing force.

Your weight and the bicycle's weight push down on the parts of the tyres that touch the ground. This force squashes the tyres, making them flatter.

To turn the bicycle, you push on one handlebar and pull on the other. These pushing and pulling forces are made by the muscles in your arms. They make the front wheel turn from side to side.

To stop the bicycle, you pull on the brake handles. Your arms make this pulling force.

To pump up your tyres, you push and pull on the pump's handle. The pushing force squeezes air into your tyres.

The brake blocks push against the wheel when you pull on the brake handles. They make a force which slows the wheel.

Your push on the pedals makes the front cog turn round. The cog makes a pulling force on the chain. In turn, the chain pulls on the back cog, making the back wheel turn.

Types of force

Every force is either a push or a pull. But these pushes and pulls are caused by different things, such as your muscles, or magnets. And forces have different effects, such as making objects move or breaking them apart.

Touching forces

Many forces are made by touching. When you throw a ball, you have to touch it to make a pushing force. When you cycle, you have to touch the pedals to make a pushing force. To lift a box, you have to touch it underneath to make a pulling force.

There are some other types of force that work by touching. Friction tries to stop things sliding against each other when they are touching. And upthrust, which is the force that makes things float, only works when things are in the water. You can find out about friction on pages 34–37 and floating on pages 38–39.

Forces can make things move along, spin round and change shape.

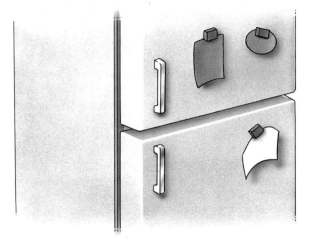

What do forces do?

To find out what forces can do, try experimenting with a pencil eraser. Push it and pull it. Push in different places. Pull in different places. Push and pull at the same time. Use two pushes, or two pulls. Use hard pushes and light pushes. What happens in each case? Try to work out why it happens. You will find that forces can make things move along, spin round and change shape.

No touching needed

There are some types of force which can make pushes and pulls without the objects touching. **Gravity** is the force that pulls us to the Earth. **Magnets** pull on metal things which are close by. Find out about gravity on pages 20–23 and magnetism on pages 24–25.

On the move

Things don't start moving on their own. They always need a force to get them going. Objects such as toy cars, pencils, balloons and balls all stay still until you move them by pushing or pulling them with your hands. Bikes, cars and trains don't go until they are moved by the force from their engines or by pedal power. So one thing a force can do is make things move.

Speeding up and slowing down

When something has started to move, a force can make it go faster. This is called **acceleration**. Imagine that a friend is wearing roller skates. You need to push to make your friend start moving. If you keep pushing, your friend will skate faster and faster. As soon as you stop pushing, your friend stops going any faster.

A force can also slow something down. And even stop it. You could stop your roller-skating friend by pushing in the other direction.

The skater needs a push to get going. She will keep rolling until another push slows her down.

On and on . . .

You know that something that is standing still won't move unless you give it a push. But what about something that is moving? It will keep moving until a force makes it stop. When astronauts went to the Moon, rockets pushed their spacecraft away from the Earth. Even though the rockets were switched off, the spacecraft kept going. There was nothing to slow it down.

> **A bigger force changes the speed of something more than a smaller force.**

Apollo 12 landed men on the Moon. When the lunar module landed, rocket engines slowed it down for a gentle landing.

Strong and weak

A bigger force changes the speed of something more than a smaller force. A big push would get a roller skater going fast straight away. A lighter push would get him or her going fast in the end, but you would have to keep pushing for much longer. It's the same with slowing down – you need bigger forces for slowing more quickly.

It takes much longer to stop a fast-moving car than a slow-moving car. The fast car must brake for longer. Why do you think speed limits make our roads safer?

Getting it going

Things that feel heavy are much more difficult to get moving than light things. And they are more difficult to stop. Of course, very light things only need a little force to start and stop them.

Racing cars are made from very strong but very light materials. It means they can accelerate very quickly.

An unequal race

If an Olympic sprinter raced against a flea over 100 metres, the sprinter would win easily. But who would be the fastest off the blocks? The answer is the flea! Sprinters have very powerful leg muscles for accelerating out of their starting blocks very quickly. A flea has very tiny leg muscles which produce only a tiny force. But the flea is so light that it can accelerate more quickly than the sprinter. However, the sprinter has a much greater top speed than the flea. Very soon he or she overtakes to win the race.

The flea is much lighter than the sprinter. It needs much less force to accelerate.

Stop!

Heavy things are difficult to get going. And once they are moving they are just as difficult to stop. Vehicles on the road need brakes that can stop them quickly in an emergency. The larger the vehicle, the stronger the brakes they need. Bicycles are light and need only small brakes. Trucks need powerful mechanical brakes to slow them down quickly.

An oil supertanker with a full load of oil is so heavy that it can take several kilometres to slow to a stop by itself.

> **Heavy things are difficult to get going. And once they are moving they are just as difficult to stop.**

Isaac Newton

Isaac Newton was a great scientist. He was born in England in 1642 and studied at Cambridge University. Isaac Newton was one of the first scientists to understand forces and how things move. He wrote down three laws of motion. Newton also explained gravity, the force which pulls everything to the ground. For more about gravity, see pages 20–23.

Forces in pairs

Imagine that you are in a swimming pool. To get yourself moving, you push off from the side. When you push, you make a force which is trying to move the side of the pool. But the pool doesn't move. *You* move instead. So where does the force that makes you move come from? The answer is that the side of the pool pushes at you. It's because forces come in pairs – your push and the pool's push are a pair.

> Forces always come in pairs. If you make one force, there will always be another pushing back.

Equals and opposites

Forces always come in pairs. If you make one force, there will always be another pushing back. Your force is called the **action**. The force that pushes back is called the **reaction**. The reaction is always the same size as your force, but it pushes in the opposite direction. The bigger the push you make, the bigger the reaction. So the harder you push the side of a swimming pool, the harder it pushes you back, and the faster you move off.

A swimmer pushes with the legs on the side of the pool to start off. The reaction from the wall makes her move.

Making a catch

Catching a ball is another example of forces acting in pairs. To stop a moving ball, you need to use a force. The force comes from the palm of your hand pushing on the ball. You can feel the reaction. It's the force that you feel pushing your hand backwards as you make the catch.

Falling-in force

Can you see the pair of forces in this picture? The person getting out of the boat pushes on it. The reaction pushes him towards the shore. This makes the boat drift away from the shore.

Adding forces

You know what happens when one force pushes or pulls something. But normally there is not just one force. There may be two forces, or three forces, or more. There might be a large pull in one direction and a small pull in another direction. How can we work out what happens in that case? The answer is that we add together the forces. So that we can add up forces, we need a way to write them down.

Force arrows

Two things make up a force. The first part is its size, which shows how strong its pull or push is. The second part is its direction, which shows which way it

pushes or pulls. We can write down a force as an arrow. The length of the arrow shows the size of the force, and the way it points shows the direction of the force.

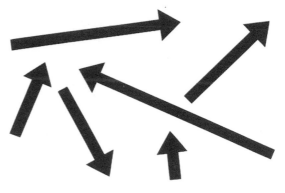

These arrows show forces of different strengths pulling and pushing in different directions. Which are strong? Which are weak?

Pulling on the lead

Each child makes a different pulling force on the lead. When two children pull, their forces are added together, making a larger force. This is shown by the longer arrow.

Two things make up a force: size and direction

Arrow adding

Adding two forces together using arrows is quite easy. First, you draw an arrow for one of the forces. Then, starting at the end of that arrow, draw an arrow for the second force. Now draw an arrow from the start of the first arrow to the end of the second arrow. This arrow shows the size and direction of the force made by adding the others together.

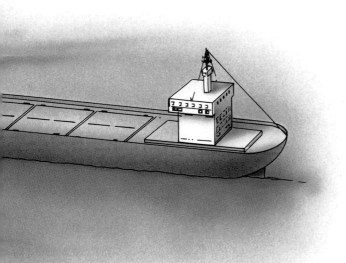

The pulls of the tugs add together to make the force pulling the ship.

Equal forces

Often, when forces are pushing and pulling on an object, the forces cancel each other out. When all the forces are added up they come to nothing. This means that the object does not start, stop, speed up or slow down. So even if an object is not moving, it does not mean that there are no forces, but that the forces acting on it are cancelling each other out. This is called *equilibrium*.

When an object is not moving, all the forces acting on it must cancel each other out.

These two children are pulling on each end of a cracker. They are pulling with the same force, but in opposite directions. The two pulls cancel each other out, so the cracker does not move. But what does happen to it?

Everything in equilibrium

All the things on the Earth are pulled downwards by the force of gravity. That includes you. Gravity is what makes you feel heavy. You feel the force as your weight. When you are sitting on a chair, your weight pushes down on the seat. Remember that every force has a reaction. So the seat pushes up on you. There are two forces on you, gravity pulling you down and the force from the chair pushing you up. The forces are the same, so they balance each other out and you don't move. You can find out more about gravity on pages 20–23.

If the seat was taken away, there would only be one force left. The person would fall to the ground.

Sailing equilibrium

When an object is not moving, all the forces acting on it must cancel each other out. And when something is moving, but not speeding up or slowing down, the forces on it cancel each other out too. A sailing boat is pushed along by the force of the wind pushing on the sails. The water flowing past the hull tries to slow the boat down. The push of the sails and the pull of the water balance each other.

*The force from the water trying to slow the boat is called **drag**. You can find out more about drag on pages 36–37.*

Squashing and stretching

As well as changing how things move, forces can squash or stretch things. They can change the shape of an object. You can stretch an elastic band by pulling at each end. And you can squeeze a sponge by pushing its sides.

How much something stretches depends on what it's made of.

The chest expander stretches because the bodybuilder is pulling on each end.

Longer and longer

The more you pull the ends of an elastic band, the longer it gets. So the bigger the force trying to stretch something, the more it stretches. But some things, such as a pencil, don't seem to stretch, however much you pull on their ends. In fact, they do stretch. But only a tiny amount – too little to see. How much something stretches depends on what it's made of. Some materials go back to their original size when the force stretching or squashing them is released. Some don't. They stay the shape they are and their shape is permanently changed.

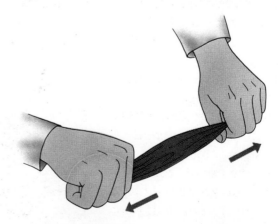

The further you stretch rubber, the bigger the pull you need. What happens when the stretching force is released?

Snap!

Things don't go on stretching for ever. When the force gets too big, they break. Some materials break very easily. Others need a huge force to break them.

Bending something stretches it on one side and squashes it on the other. Bending it too much makes the material split apart.

Using stretching and squashing

We can use things that squash and stretch to our advantage. Elastic bands are a good example. You can stretch them around a bundle of things, then release the stretching force so that the elastic band gets shorter again and holds the bundle together. Metal springs are similar. They are used in hundreds of machines.

A spring in a motorcycle

Turning forces

As we've seen, a force can make an object start or stop, speed it up or slow it down, and make it change direction. By pushing or pulling an object in the right place, you can also make it turn round. Think about how you make a gyroscope spin round. The string pulls at the side of the gyroscope's central spindle. A force that makes an object spin round is called a *turning force*.

> **By pushing or pulling an object in the right place, you can make it turn round.**

The fulcrum

An important place on a turning object is called the **fulcrum**. It's the point around which the object turns. A see-saw uses turning forces. The fulcrum of a see-saw is the pivot in the middle.

Your weight on the see-saw makes the see-saw turn up and down on its pivot. Your weight is the turning force.

Larger forces

The further away from the fulcrum a force is, the greater its turning effect. A door is another example of a turning object. The fulcrum is the hinged side of the door. Try opening a door by pushing it a few centimetres away from the hinge. You have to push very hard. Pushing on the other side, using the handle, is much easier. You are pushing further away from the fulcrum, so the turning effect is much greater.

Nº 22. *Le Borda.* Les élèves au cabestan.

A capstan was used to raise a ship's anchor. The long poles made the work easier.

Going round and going along

Starting to spin an object and stopping it spinning is just like starting and stopping it moving along. You just have to push or pull in a different place. The effect of the force is the same too. To speed up an object you need to give it a push. To make it go more quickly, you need to give it a harder push. It's the same with spinning. To increase the object's spinning speed takes a push. A harder push makes it spin faster still. A heavy object needs a bigger push to get it moving than a light object. It also needs a bigger push to get it spinning.

To turn a roundabout, you have to push sideways at the edge. Pushing in or out has no effect.

Gravity 1

There is one force that pulls on every object on the Earth all the time. It's the force of gravity. Gravity is what makes things fall to the ground. We feel the force of gravity pulling on objects. It's what we call *weight*. Gravity always pulls towards the middle of the Earth, and unlike the forces we've seen so far, it works without touching anything.

The saying 'What goes up must come down' depends on gravity. The athlete jumps up, but is pulled back down by gravity.

The packing material is bigger than the hi-fi unit, but much lighter. It has much less matter in it.

Mass and weight

All things are made up of what we call matter. Some objects have lots of matter in them and some have only a bit. The amount of matter that makes up an object is called its **mass**. The more matter an object has, the greater its mass. The mass of something depends on what it's made of and how big it is. Mass is measured in units called **grams** and **kilograms**.

The force of gravity pulling an object down depends on its mass. The bigger the mass, the bigger the force. So objects with a big mass feel heavy.

What makes gravity?

Every object is pulled towards every other object by gravity. Your pencil is pulled towards you, and you are pulled towards your pencil. This book is pulled towards you, and you are pulled towards it. The pencil and book also attract each other. But the force of gravity between two objects depends on how heavy they are. The force between even quite large things, such as two cars, is far too small to notice. It needs an object as big as the Earth to make gravity noticeable.

Gravity always pulls towards the middle of the Earth.

Gravity holds everything down on the Earth. It even keeps the atmosphere in place.

Galileo

Galileo was a famous Italian scientist. He lived from 1564 to 1642. Galileo was the first person to notice that when you drop two objects of different weights from a height, they hit the ground together. Many people thought that heavier objects fall faster than light ones. But although the force of gravity on a heavy object is greater, it needs a bigger force to get it moving, so it falls in the same way as a light object. Galileo made many other discoveries, including the fact that the Earth goes around the Sun.

Gravity 2

The force of gravity between two objects gradually gets weaker as the objects move further apart. Mountaineers weigh a tiny bit less when they are on the world's tallest mountains because they are slightly further away from the centre of the Earth where gravity is slightly weaker. But gravity still works over huge distances if the objects are big enough. The Earth and the Moon are attracted to each other by gravity. This pull keeps the Moon in orbit around the Earth.

> The force of gravity between two objects gradually gets weaker as the objects move further apart.

Gravity keeps the Moon in orbit around the Earth. The same happens with the Sun and the Earth.

One of the Apollo astronauts played golf on the Moon. Scientists estimate that you could hit a golf ball 1.6 kilometres on the Moon, compared with about 300 metres on Earth.

Gravity on the Moon

The astronauts who landed on the Moon weighed less while they were there. In fact, they only weighed about one-sixth of what they weighed on Earth. The reason is that the Moon's mass is only about one-sixth that of the Earth. Remember that the astronauts' mass stayed the same. Only their weight changed.

Gravity and tides

There are gravitational forces between the Moon and Sun, and water in the Earth's oceans. These forces are very tiny, but because the oceans are so huge, their effect is noticed. As the Earth spins, the direction of the gravitational pull on different parts of the world changes. This makes the water slowly 'slosh' about in the oceans. At the shores, the level of the water goes up and down, making tides.

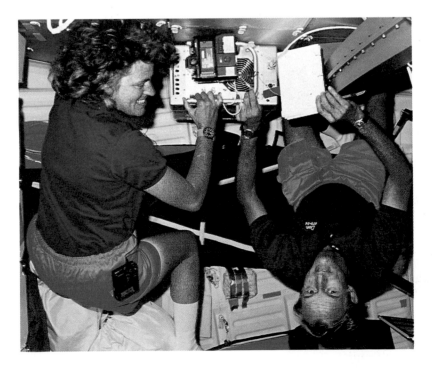

Weightlessness

When astronauts are in orbit around the Earth, they float about inside their spacecraft. They feel weightless, as though there was no gravity. This is because they and their spacecraft are orbiting the Earth together at the same speed. In fact, the spacecraft and the astronauts are all held in orbit by the Earth's gravity. Without it, they would float off into space.

Magnetism

We've already seen how the force of gravity works even between different planets millions of kilometres apart. Another force that works without touching is the force of magnetism.

Magnetic forces

Magnetism only works between two magnets, or between a magnet and certain metal objects. The most common magnetic metal is iron. Things that contain iron, like steel, also work. There is always a force of attraction between a magnet and a piece of iron. But with two magnets, there can be attraction and repulsion. It depends on which part of the magnets you bring close together.

All magnets have two areas on them where the magnetic force is strongest. They are called the **north pole** and the **south pole**. The south poles of different magnets **repel** each other. So do the north poles. But south and north **attract** each other. The strength of the attracting or repelling force gets stronger and stronger as the magnets get closer.

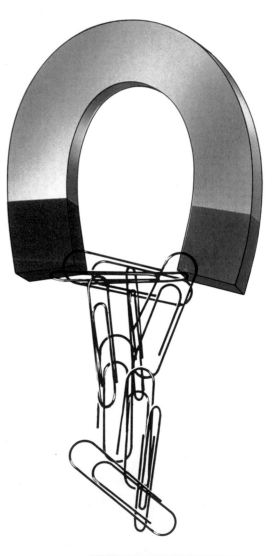

Remember the rule: like poles repel and opposite poles attract.

Using magnetic forces

Magnets are convenient for temporary
fixings, such as magnetic message
holders and door catches.
The most important use
of magnets is in
electric motors.
Electric motors use
electromagnets.
These are
magnets made
by passing
electricity
through coils
of wire.
Electromagnets
are useful
because they
can be turned on
and off. Also,
their poles can be
swapped round by
changing the direction
of the electric current.
Electromagnets produce the
forces which turn the motor.

*Electric motors turn magnetic forces into
forces which turn drill bits and train wheels.*

Electric forces

The force that attracts
your hair to a comb is
another type of force that
works without contact. It
is an electric force. It
works between positive
and negative electric
charges. Like the magnetic
force, it can attract and
repel – opposite charges
attract and like charges
repel.

Measuring forces

Sometimes it is useful to measure how strong a force is. Then we can compare forces with each other, and work out mathematically what effect they will have. Knowing the size of forces is very important in engineering, for example. To measure a force, we look at the effect it has on something – for example, how much it stretches a spring. The force that we measure most often is an object's weight.

Newtons

Just as we measure length in metres and time in hours and minutes, so we measure forces in units called **newtons**. But how big is a newton? Well, the force of gravity on a 100 gram bar of chocolate is about one newton. So if you hold a 100 gram object in your hand, the force pressing on your palm is about one newton.

How many newtons?

You can measure the strength of a force by looking at what effect the force has. The simplest force-measuring device is a **force meter**. Inside is a spring that is

You can compare the weights of things by feeling the force they make on your hands.

We measure force in units called newtons.

stretched by the force pulling on it. The pointer is attached to the spring and moves along the scale. The bigger the force, the more the spring stretches.

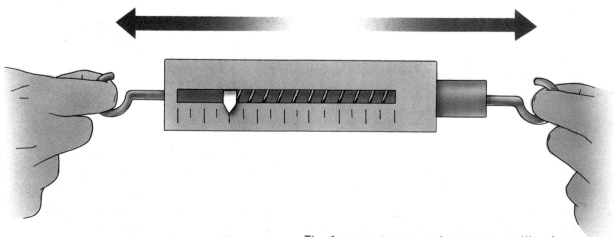

The force meter can only measure pulling forces.

Weighing machines

A weighing machine is a special force-measuring device. It measures the force of gravity pulling an object towards the Earth. However, the scale on the machine does not show force, but mass. It measures kilograms. The machine automatically works out what mass would make the force it measures.

The weight in the pan stretches the spring inside the scale.

A balance with a set of weights. One or more weights are used to measure the weights of different objects.

Balances

A balance is a weighing machine that measures a force by balancing it with a known force. The most common type of balance consists of an arm resting on a central fulcrum. The object to be weighed hangs on one side. Known weights are added to the other side. When the arm is level, the forces trying to turn it each way are the same. So the weight being measured is the same as the total of all the weights on the other side.

Forces and energy

Energy makes things happen. You need energy to make your body work and to make your muscles move. That energy comes from the food you eat. A car needs energy to move along. That energy is stored in its *fuel*. Whenever a force makes an object move or change shape, energy is needed. The energy comes from the thing that makes the force. That's why you get tired as you ride your bike – you use up your energy making forces.

> When a force makes an object move or change shape, energy is needed.

Where does energy come from?

When a force makes an object move or change shape, energy is needed. But where does that energy come from? Imagine giving a friend on a sledge a good push to get him or her going. You are making the force to start the sledge moving, so the energy must come from you. A bit of the energy stored in your body is used up.

If you keep pushing the sledge, you run out of energy. You can replace the energy by eating some food.

Where does energy go?

Energy comes in many different forms, and it can change from one form to another. But it can never disappear. So when you push your friend on the sledge, the energy you use to make the pushing force must go somewhere. In fact, it is turned into **movement energy**. Movement energy is energy that things have because they are moving. The faster an object is going and the heavier it is, the more movement energy it has.

You need to apply a force to a book to put it on a shelf. So you use energy. The energy is stored because the book has moved to a higher position.

Storing energy

When a force squashes or stretches an object, the energy needed to make the squashing or stretching force gets stored in the object. For example, if you stretch an elastic band, you use energy to stretch it. The energy is stored in the elastic band. If you let the elastic band go, the energy is released. It creates a force which pulls your hands back together.

The energy to fire an arrow comes from the food the archer eats. The energy is used by muscles to bend the bow. The energy in the bent bow is then turned into movement energy in the arrow.

Resisting forces

How do we resist the force of gravity pulling all the things in a skyscraper to the ground? How does a tent stay up in a gale? The answer is that we design these force-resisting structures correctly. That means knowing what forces do to a structure, what materials to use and how to join them together strongly.

Buildings resist forces by having a sturdy structure.

Buildings

Buildings are much larger and more complicated than park benches, but they resist forces in the same way. The force that a building resists is the weight of all the people, furniture and fittings in it. The structure of the building transfers the weight from the floors down into the ground. Buildings with more than two or three floors have a strong concrete or steel frame which carries the weight. Out of sight under the building are foundations to spread the weight into the ground.

Taking the weight

A simple example of a structure which resists the force of gravity is a bench. When you sit in the middle of the bench, the bench holds your weight. Your weight pushing down in the centre of the bench is carried along to the legs and down into the ground. The bench does not move, but it does change shape slightly by bending. The thinner the bench, the more it will bend. The seat is thick enough not to bend too much, but not so thick that it wastes wood.

The steel frame in a skyscraper bends very slightly under the weight. It also sways slightly in strong winds.

Resisting forces slowly

Buildings resist forces by having a sturdy structure. But sometimes it is better to resist forces with a structure that changes shape a lot. This sort of structure helps to reduce the chance of injury in road accidents. Most modern cars have built-in 'crumple' zones at the front. If a car with a solid front hits a wall, it stops very quickly. The occupants could be thrown out of the car. A crumple zone collapses as the car hits the wall. The car slows down gradually, with less chance of injury to the passengers.

A crumple zone acts like a cushion, reducing the force of impact. Another example of a collapsing structure is a crash barrier along the roadside.

Moving in circles

Imagine spinning round in a circle with a heavy bag in your outstretched hand. The bag moves in a large circle around you. It keeps going at the same speed, but to get round the circle, the bag has to keep changing direction. You know that to make an object start or stop, or to change its speed and direction, you need a force. That means that there must be a force making the bag change direction. And because the bag is moving all the time, the force must be there all the time.

Into the middle

As you are spinning your bag around, what happens to your arm? You should feel a pull trying to stretch it. And because forces come in pairs, if the bag is pulling on you, then you must be pulling on the bag. Your pull is the force that keeps the bag moving in its circle. It's always the same – to make an object move in a circle you need a force towards the centre of the circle. And the faster you spin round and the heavier the bag, the bigger the force that you need.

Here's another example of moving in a circle. When the thrower releases the hammer, it stops moving in a circle and goes off in a straight line.

> To make an object move in a circle you need a force towards the centre of the circle.

Going round the bend

Anything that goes round a bend needs a force pointing into the bend to make it turn. To turn a corner, a bird tilts its wings to one side. This makes some of the lifting force from its wings point inwards, so the bird turns.

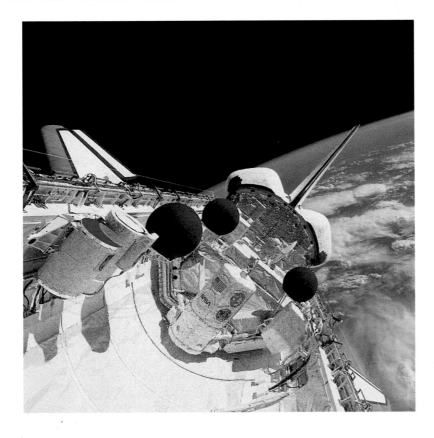

Into orbit

Objects in orbit, such as satellites and space stations, are moving in a huge circle around the Earth. So there must be a force pulling them towards the centre of the Earth. That force is gravity. Without gravity, they would simply drift off into space.

To reach an orbit just outside the Earth's atmosphere, like the one this space shuttle is in, a spacecraft needs to travel at a speed of about 28,000 kilometres per hour.

Friction 1

Why do you have to keep pushing a book to keep it sliding across a desk? And what makes your hands warm when you rub them together? The answer is *friction*. Friction tries to stop things sliding against each other. Friction is the force that stops a book moving if you only push it lightly. And friction slows the book to a stop when it is moving.

Friction tries to stop things sliding against each other.

The force of friction between the cover of the book and the top of the desk slows down the book. To keep the book moving, you have to keep pushing.

What causes friction?

The rougher two surfaces are, the greater the force of friction between them. Friction also gets bigger as the force pushing the surfaces together gets greater. If you rest the palm of your hand lightly on a table top it is easy to slide it about. But press down and it becomes very difficult to move. Now put a sheet of paper between your hand and the table. The paper will slide easily because it is much smoother than your hand.

Even surfaces that look smooth can cause friction. Under a microscope you can see the tiny bumps in the surface.

Heating up

You can warm up your hands by rubbing them together. The heat is caused by friction between the palms of your hands. The harder you push your hands together and the faster you rub, the warmer your hands get.

Friction between the match and the striking panel on the side of the box makes the heat needed to ignite the match.

Fighting friction

In machines that have components which move rapidly against each other, such as car engines, friction creates problems. In an engine, friction tries to slow the moving parts, and it causes unwanted heat. This wastes fuel and means there is a danger of the parts melting. To reduce friction, we use lubricants, such as engine oil.

Skis have a coating of wax on their undersides to reduce friction between the skis and the snow.

Friction 2

We've seen that friction tries to stop things sliding against each other. Friction between the moving parts in the wheel and pedal bearings tries to slow down your bike. But there is another type of friction which means that however hard you push on the pedals, you can't go above a certain speed. It's caused by the air that you are riding through. It is called *drag*.

The force of the wind

The force of drag trying to slow you down when you cycle along is exactly the same as the force of the wind that bends trees and tries to blow you over on windy days. If you cycle along at 30 kilometres an hour on a still day, the drag trying to slow you down is the same as the force you would feel if you stood still in a 30 kilometre per hour wind. The faster you cycle, the greater the drag becomes. In fact, in the end, it gets so large that you can't go any faster, however hard you push on the pedals.

Drag happens because you have to push through the air to move along.

A bob sleigh has a streamlined body to reduce drag as much as possible. The crew also duck their heads out of the airflow.

Streamlining

What difference in shape is there between fast sports cars and cars for use around town? Fast cars always have a smooth body shape, specially designed so that the air can flow smoothly past as the car speeds along. This is called streamlining. It reduces drag, so that the car has a greater top speed. Streamlining also helps to reduce fuel consumption. Town cars don't need to go very fast, so streamlining isn't so important.

Drag doesn't just happen in air. It slows things down in all gases and liquids. Streamlining is just as important if you want to travel fast under water. The sail fish is the fastest fish in the sea.

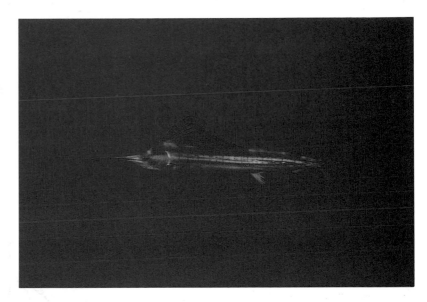

Drag doesn't just happen in air. It slows things down in all gases and liquids.

Getting hotter

Objects that travel through the air very fast, such as **supersonic** aeroplanes, get very hot on the outside. This is caused by the air rubbing against the outside. The outside of the space shuttle is heated to over 1000°C as it re-enters the Earth's atmosphere after a mission.

When a meteorite falls into the Earth's atmosphere, it burns up, making a streak of light.

Floating and sinking

Why do things float? It's for the same reason that a chair keeps you above the ground. Just as the chair pushes you up to balance the force of gravity pulling you down, the water pushes up to balance the weight of the floating object. You can feel this upward force if you try to push an empty plastic bottle or a hollow ball under the water. The force is called *upthrust*.

How big is upthrust?

Upthrust always pushes upwards, trying to push things out of the water. The size of the upthrust on an object depends on the amount of water pushed out of the way. The further you push an empty bottle into the water, the bigger the force you need to keep it there because it moves more and more water out of the way. Do you think upthrust depends on weight?

Try pushing different objects under the water to see how big the upthrust on them is.

How things float

The further an object goes into the water, the more water it pushes out of the way, and the greater the upthrust becomes. When the upthrust equals the weight of the object, the two forces cancel each other out and the object floats. If the object is completely under water and the upthrust is still not equal to its weight, the object sinks.

A light ball floats with only a tiny part under the water.

An iceberg floats with only a tiny part above the water.

When the upthrust equals the weight of the object, the object floats. If the upthrust is less than the weight, the object sinks.

A submarine dives by filling its ballast tanks with water. This makes it heavier, so that upthrust cannot keep it floating. How do you think it surfaces again?

Archimedes

Archimedes was a Greek mathematician, physicist and inventor. He was born in about 287BC. Archimedes invented many mechanical devices and worked out some important mathematical laws. He is probably most famous for being the first person to understand about upthrust. It is said that the idea came to him while he was in the bath. He leapt out and ran around shouting 'Eureka!', which means 'I have found it!'.

Machines

When you hear the word 'machine' you might think of complicated things, such as washing machines or building-site diggers. However, any device that makes a job easier by changing the force needed to do it is a machine. Machines can be very simple devices, such as pliers, tin openers and screwdrivers. Pliers let you grip small things more tightly than you could with your fingers. A screwdriver makes it easier to turn a screw.

> Any device that makes a job easier by changing the force needed to do it is a machine.

Levers

A lever is a simple machine which consists of a bar that turns around a fixed point. The fixed point is called the **fulcrum.** Pulling or pushing on one part of the lever makes it turn around the fulcrum and produce a force at another part of the lever.

A lever can be used to lift a weight. The further away from the fulcrum the person pushes, the smaller the force needed to lift the weight.

Back-to-front levers

The push or pull that you use to operate a lever is called the **effort**, and the force that it produces is called the **load**. The load and effort do not have to be on opposite sides of the fulcrum. Sometimes, instead of the load being nearer the fulcrum than the effort, it is the other way round.

In a pair of nutcrackers and a pair of tweezers, the fulcrum is at the end. Instead of increasing force, tweezers reduce it, so that you can pick up delicate things without damaging them.

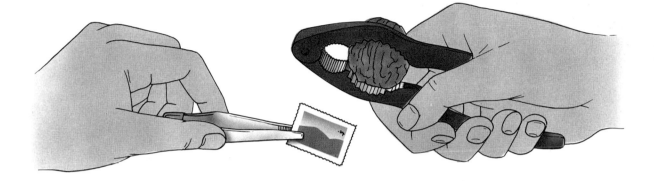

More machines

A ramp is a sort of machine. The force needed to push the weight up the ramp is much less than the force that would be needed to lift it vertically.

On yachts, pulleys are used to haul in and raise sails. A pulley reduces the force needed to move an object at the end of a rope. The more turns of rope there are in a pulley, the smaller the force needed.

Pressure

Pressure is the amount of force that presses on a certain area. If you make the force on an area bigger, you increase the pressure on the area. Making the area smaller and keeping the force the same also increases the pressure.

The pressure at a sharp point is very great. This post has a sharp point at the bottom end which makes it easier to push the post into the ground.

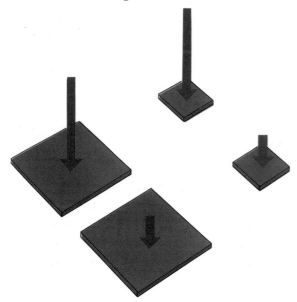

Pressure is the amount of force that presses on a certain area.

Changing pressure

High pressure can be a nuisance or an advantage. Wide tyres reduce pressure. They help to stop vehicles sinking into mud or snow. Tracks on vehicles do the same job. Walking in deep snow is made easier by wearing snow shoes. They spread a person's weight over a much bigger area than normal shoes. Pressure can be increased by making the area that the force presses on smaller.

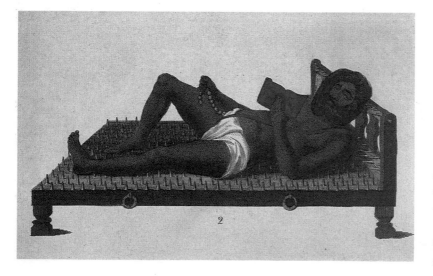

Lying on a bed of nails is painful, but not as dangerous as it looks. Although the points are sharp, there are hundreds of them. Spreading the weight over all the points reduces the pressure.

Pressure under water

The weight of an object pushes down on the surface it is resting on. This causes pressure on the surface. Imagine that object is replaced by a block of water. There would still be pressure. This is what happens under the water. The further down into the water you go, the bigger the weight of water above you, and the greater the pressure is. The difference under water is that the pressure pushes down, up and sideways as well. In fact, it pushes in all directions.

The pressure under the sea soon gets very high. The deepest a diver can safely go is about 120 metres under the surface. Any deeper and the pressure would begin to crush the diver's body.

Air pressure

The weight of the air in the atmosphere also causes pressure. Air pressure gradually reduces as you go up into the atmosphere. The air also gets thinner.

When you are on the Earth's surface, it is like being at the bottom of a lake of air. When you breathe in, air pressure forces the air into your lungs.

Above about 4000 metres above sea level, the air is very thin. There is less oxygen than lower down. Breathing during exercise is difficult.

Glossary

Acceleration When an object gets faster or slower (changes speed), it accelerates. Objects that change direction also accelerate.

Attraction Pulling together.

Brake A device used to slow down a vehicle. Brakes work using friction.

Cog A disc with teeth around the outside. Cogs are used in many machines.

Drag A force which tries to stop objects moving through a liquid or a gas.

Effort The force used to make a machine move a load.

Electric force The force between two electrically charged particles.

Electromagnet A magnet made by passing electric current through a coil of wire.

Equilibrium When two or more forces cancel each other out they are in equilibrium.

Force A push or a pull on an object. The size of a force is measured in newtons.

Force meter A device used to measure the size of a force.

Friction The force between things trying to slide past each other. It stops the things sliding or tries to slow them down.

Fuel A substance which is burned to make energy, such as food or petrol.

Fulcrum The place around which an object turns, such as the pivot of a see-saw.

Gram A unit of mass. There are 100 grams in a kilogram.

Gravity The force that pulls all objects towards each other. It is only noticeable when one of the objects has a huge mass (such as a planet).

Hydraulic machine A machine that uses a liquid to work is a hydraulic machine.

Lever A machine consisting of a bar that turns around a fixed point.

Load The force that a machine overcomes.

Machine A device that makes a job easier by changing a force.

Magnet A piece of magnetic material. Magnets attract or repel other magnets and some metals.

Magnetism The way some materials attract or repel each other without touching.

Mass The amount of matter in an object. Mass is measured in kilograms.

Movement energy The energy that things have because they are moving.

Newton The unit used to measure the size of a force.

Orbit The path that a satellite takes around a planet. Most orbits are ellipses (like a squashed circle).

Pneumatic machine A machine that uses air to work is called a pneumatic machine.

Poles The two areas on a magnet (called the north and south poles) where the magnetism is strongest.

Pressure The amount of force pressing on a certain area.

Pulley A machine made from a system of ropes and wheels, often used to lift heavy weights.

Reaction Forces come in pairs. Every force, or **action**, has another force pushing back, called the reaction.

Repulsion Pushing apart.

Speed How fast an object moves.

Spring A strip of wire twisted into a spiral. Springs can be stretched or compressed and will return to their original shape.

Streamlining The shaping of an object to reduce its drag.

Supersonic Faster than the speed that sound travels in the atmosphere.

Turning force A force that makes an object spin round.

Unit A measurement, such as metre (a unit of length), kilogram (a unit of weight) and newton (a unit of force).

Upthrust The force pushing upwards on an object which is in a liquid or a gas. Upthrust makes things float.

Weight The weight of something is how much gravity pulls it downwards. Weight is a force.

Index

Published by BBC Educational Publishing,
BBC White City, 201 Wood Lane,
London W12 7TS

First Published 1994
© Chris Oxdale/BBC Enterprises Ltd 1994
The moral right of the author has been asserted.

Paperback ISBN: 0 563 39654 7
Hardback ISBN: 0 563 39783 7

Colour reproduction by Daylight Colour, Singapore
Cover origination in England by Goodfellow and Egan
Printed and bound in England by BPC, Paulton

Photo credits:

Allsport **pp. 8, 10, 15, 20, 32, 35, 36;** Berken of Cowes (UK) **p. 41 (right);** BBC/John Green **pp. 2/3, 25, 27, 40;** John Cleare/Mountain Camera **p. 43 (bottom);** Lupe Cunha **p. 18;** Mary Evans Picture Library **pp. 19, 42 (bottom);** Ford Motor Company **p. 31 (bottom);** Sally and Richard Greenhill **p. 41 (left);** Robert Harding Picture Library **pp. 16, 29, 31 (top), 45;** NASA **p. 33 (bottom);** NASA/Science Photo Library **pp. 22, 23;** National Trust Photographic Library/Robert Thrift **p. 42 (top);** Network/Barry Lewis **p. 28 (top);** Oxford Scientific Films **pp. 17 (top), 38;** Planet Earth Pictures **pp. 33 (top), 37 (top), 39, 43 (top);** Science Photo Library **pp. 7 (top), 21, 37 (bottom);** Shell **p. 9;** Tony Stone Images **p. 28 (bottom);** John Walmsley **pp. 7 (bottom), 44;** Zefa Pictures **p. 17 (bottom).**

Front cover: Tony Stone Images **(main picture)** blurred action shot of track runners' legs; BBC/John Green **(bottom right)** magnet and pins.